How to die well without god

Ann

Live well

Dr Bob.

How to die well without god

Robert Keats PhD.

© Robert Keats, 2017

Published by Robert Keats

A CIP catalogue record for this book is available from the British Library.

ISBN 978-0-9955790-0-2

Book layout and cover design by Clare Brayshaw

Cover image ©Azathoth973 | Dreamstime.com – The Dying Oak Photo

Prepared and printed by:

York Publishing Services Ltd
64 Hallfield Road
Layerthorpe
York YO31 7ZQ

Tel: 01904 431213

Website: www.yps-publishing.co.uk

For Helen, Holly, and Sophie

Contents

Introduction

I'd like a good death, but the two original books on 'how to die well' known as the *Ars Moriendi* or the art of dying were written in the 15th century and produced by the church to draw the dying back to god. Indeed, they stated that dying well could only be through god, and that's my problem: I don't believe in god. Allan Ropper, a neurosurgeon, in his book *Reaching down the Rabbit Hole*, noted that 'end of life, fearing the end of life, having a loved one near the end of their life: this is the foxhole that lacks atheists.' And so it does; so how is it possible to have a good death without god?

I'm a late post-war baby boomer; a generation that usually gets what it wants. The 'boomers' are now looking to take back some control of the process of dying, and many people want a good death without god. My curiosity about the topic was triggered by my own impending death from Motor Neurone Disease (MND, or ALS in the US). I've read lots of books about dying, and its associated loss and grief, and authors seem to find good stories when ruminating about the loss of a loved one or telling their own story about news of a terminal diagnosis. As I explored the cultural background behind them, the lack of a cultural anchor for those free from religion became obvious, and so this is my route map to help me achieve a final wish. I readily acknowledge some readers will not take to my thinking, and others will reject a more calculating commentary on something as emotional as death. But there is compassion even in close analysis; indeed, exploring death without belief can offer a better understanding of it.

Many years ago I worked for a company with a management mantra that included the comment 'We're all going to die, but we can die conveniently or inconveniently.' Every time I recall that quote I try to grasp the meaning of what appears to be a daft statement, but now I'm dying and think my condition inconvenient, I realise it is more convenient than many other circumstances I can imagine. On the same day recently I got news of a friend diagnosed with colon cancer, and another who'd spent three weeks in a coma after heart surgery. Perhaps my lot is not so bad. I wrote to another friend that week, saying that if I didn't have MND then I could die of something far worse. It's a bit like Monty Python's 'Four Yorkshiremen' sketch, where they try to outdo each other in their childhood miseries. Like so many of my generation I know the lines off by heart – 'We lived in a shoe box...Cardboard box? Ee, you were lucky!' – but rather than life, my sketch is about the topic of death. Conveniently, I get the chance to reflect on how others have approached death.

I aim to present an interpretation of death untainted by religious superstition, and at the same time give some useful insights for those facing death that may also help family and friends. The book is in two parts: the first part sets out the philosophical and religious underpinning of the West's traditional attitudes to death and dying; the second part gives practical advice on a good death, which I hope works for those with or without religious beliefs. Part I is philosophical and may not suit every reader, so go straight to part II if you only want the practical, personal stuff. I refer to the practices of 'the church' in this book, but my comments are about religion in general.

Chapter one considers how our view of death is made worse by the fear generated by superstition, and it sets out a philosophical position based on the ideas of Epicurus, who famously said 'death is nothing'. Chapter two explores how moral values impact on the way we live and die, and how a well-considered morality, free from religion, means old cultural and religious values need no longer be the benchmark. Chapter three builds on these views to set out a stronger symbolism for non-believers, something I call *factism*. Chapter four starts the more practical part of the book, and reviews the meaning of a good death without god. Chapter five considers the behaviours and language we use in relation to someone close to us who is dying, and specifically looks at how our communication can be improved without the fog of superstition. Chapter six looks at the implications of loss for the bereaved. Chapter seven sketches the cultural and legal options for those wanting more control over their death: through assisted dying, or support with palliative care, and chapter eight, with a hint of dark humour, is titled 'decommissioning', listing the important things to get done before you die. I've added my personal reflections after examining my life, because, as Socrates said, the unexamined life is not worth living.

I chose to go public about my disease after my diary scribblings found their way into the MND Association fora, and they coincided with promoting MND Awareness month on BBC TV news in June 2016, a year after my diagnosis. This, in turn, led to coverage on the Radio 4 *Today* programme, and a feature in my local press. By then I knew in my own mind what I was facing, and I had already arranged all my personal affairs and paid for my funeral. The work with the MND Association led me to consider how we might help others affected by death, and I hope this commentary helps a few. Don't ask me if I have all the answers; but the references at the end of the book might help you frame better questions. This is a book about death associated with terminal diseases, and is not intended for those coping with sudden or violent death. The stories told here work better for those who have time to think, reflect, and then act.

Robert Keats PhD, January 2017

PART I –

A MORAL FRAMEWORK FOR A GOOD DEATH

Superstition and the fear of death

I had a typical childhood in the 1950s. The family went to church on Sunday, and by the 1960s I was in the church choir, attending two or three Sunday services – Matins, Holy Communion, and Evensong, as well as choir practice on Wednesdays and Fridays. The singing was fun, but as a child I didn't get the religious stuff, and I still don't. Fifty years on I now want a good death, on my terms, avoiding the nonsense of religious superstition. It is not straightforward to escape religion's pervading influence; it is so deeply embedded in our Western culture it affects our language and habits, our customs and practices. A religious-free death requires some careful planning.

The *Ars Moriendi* was part of the conceptual structure built by the church to maintain its powerful grip on people's lives. That grip may now be weaker, particularly for the secular post-war baby boomers, and the message that dying well can only be through god no longer applies. It is extraordinary that the predictable and inevitable act of dying has, down the ages, been turned into a miserable tale of woe, even for those at the end of their natural lives; the church must bear responsibility for some of that misery.

I am no fan of the practices of the Christian church, but they did not invent the fear of death; which was already in play before the followers of Jesus got going. It came first (in the western tradition at least) from Greco/Roman myths, with the fear of hell, where the god Tartarus lived. Over time his name became associated with the place below ground, used originally to hold ghosts that threatened the Olympic gods, and it later became a place of punishment. It was ruled over by Hades and Persephone and, although the Greek writers Hesiod, Homer, Ovid and Plato all had slightly different versions of the myth, they all adhered to the story that ghosts had to cross the river Styx (literally the river 'hated') guarded by the three-headed dog Cerberus, and after crossing they were judged, with the virtuous offered the road to the Elysian fields and happiness, and the evil sent to the punishment fields. The Greek underworld stories have the same roots that gave us hell in the bible; for both it's a fiery place below ground. Through oral tradition, and then in writing, hell became a place of torment.

Bertrand Russell, in his 1927 speech *Why I am not a Christian*, reiterated the point. It's freely available on the internet, and is still worth a read.

> *'Religion is based primarily and mainly upon fear…*
> *Fear is the basis of the whole thing – fear of the*
> *mysterious, fear of defeat, fear of death. Fear is the*
> *parent of cruelty, and therefore it is no wonder if*
> *cruelty and religion have gone hand in hand.'*

Fear of what happens to non-believers in the so-called afterlife was a significant element of the church's power, and it became accepted practice to use this fear for everyday threats to the general population. In the medieval period the Christian church turned hell into an even darker place through such works as Dante's *Divine Comedy*, a brilliant but scary piece of imaginative writing that set the scene for depicting hell in modern times. As an example: there's a favourite choral piece with a lovely tune and the words from the burial service, 'deliver us not into the bitter pains of eternal death.' It isn't calculated to make you want to die soon, and it aligns with the hideous practice of burying unbaptised children and suicides outside consecrated ground, because they had died without god. The narrator in Robert Harris's novel *An Officer and a Spy* calls the church a 'superstition factory' and retired Bishop John Shelby Spong said, back in 2006, that the church was 'in the guilt producing control process.' For me, there is little doubt that religion preys upon the fears and discomfort of those who are dying, and it affects those who care for them as well. It can readily be argued it's a disproportionate fear; and yet the story could have been so very different.

Even as the Greeks were formalising their myths there were different stories being told. Epicurus, a Greek philosopher, developed a very different narrative, which is more rational and free from fear. Born in 341 BCE on the island of Samos, near the Turkish coast, he moved to Athens soon after Socrates died. He knew, as did all thoughtful people of his time, that the early Greek myths, such as those written by Hesiod some 500 years earlier, were simply made up – an act of creative poetry. It was part of the artistic effort to explain how the world was formed from Chaos (literally chasm); this poetry gave rise to simple creation stories, such as Prometheus making man from clay and water. In Epicurus' time the myths still lacked any commonly agreed format, and so the gods were more like good luck charms. Importantly, because there was no custom of slavishly following religious creeds, he chose to dismiss the gods. At that time monotheism was only just emerging, but he was already critical of the idea of the shift from many gods to a single deity, and in response he said:

> *Is God willing to prevent evil, but not able? Then he is not omnipotent.*
> *Is he able, but not willing? Then he is malevolent.*
> *Is he both able and willing? Then whence cometh evil?*
> *Is he neither able nor willing? Then why call him God?*

My research supports the last line here, and although Epicurus' use of the word god was translated with a capital 'G' there is no evidence for giving any god credit for a capital 'G' more generally in this book.

Epicurus' teachings were readily available to educated Romans, but a lot of his work was suppressed – and texts actually lost – in the period after the Christian church was established. The Roman Emperor Justinian closed down his school in Athens (albeit 800 years after it was established). In the 15th century a major work by the Epicurean Roman poet Lucretius (99 BCE – c. 55 BCE) was rediscovered in a German monastery, and it then became possible to piece together a more comprehensive picture of his work. The clarity displayed by Epicurus is impressive; he was exploring the limit of human knowledge in an effort to overcome uncertainty, and he carefully worked through the available evidence. In matters of science he was an atomist (atom literally meaning 'un-splittable'), and his work influenced the thinking of people like John Locke and Isaac Newton.

In reply to Epicurus' proposition that the soul died with the body – it was just another organ of the body, and it dissolved on death – the Jews said the Epicureans would not enjoy life after death. This despite their own Torah, also replicated the Christian book of Genesis, agreeing with the Greek view of 'dust to dust'. Only three of Epicurus' actual letters were saved, including one to his friend Menoeceus, which included the following:

> *Death, therefore, the most awful of evils, is nothing to us, seeing that, when we are, death is not come, and, when death is come, we are not.*

Here Epicurus focuses on the moment of death, nothing more. Henry Scott Holland wrote a poem and book in 1909 with a similar title, and it is possible to see Epicurus as one influence for the opening of the poem:

> *Death is nothing at all.*
> *I have only slipped away to the next room.*

Scott Holland starts off well, but from the second line he shifts to the well-trodden path of religious sentiment, and he ends his poem saying:

> *One brief moment and all will be as it was before only better,*
> *infinitely happier and forever we will all be one together with Christ.*

The poem manages to shift from Epicurean teaching in the first line to belief in a Christian afterlife by the end.

It worries me that this poem, and hundreds like it, give mixed messages without any underpinning justification. They offer a sweet afterlife at the same time as the church peddles real fear. It further increases uncertainty and anxiety for those who are dying and it's easy to find evidence of that uncertainty in people's thinking. The internet offers lots of websites giving advice on death. Here's one comment from the Healthtalk website:

> *Well, I mean, I'm not religious. But I do have this sort of feeling that God's forsaken me. And I know that's a horrible thing to say, because people die all the time and God can't save everybody. But I sort of think, 'Oh, he's sort of given up on me a bit.' And so I'm certainly not a religious person. So where do I draw the strength from?*

People in this frame of mind already find it difficult to manage their own circumstances, and any ambiguity about god just makes things worse. The suggestion that god can't save everybody is as unhelpful as it is irrational; not because a deity should be able to save everyone, but because it is based on superstition in the first place, and the idea that a deity gives up on people is equally irrational for the same reasons. This book looks to answer the last sentence from the quote – where people with no belief, or uncertain belief, can go to draw strength.

People facing death need a clarity far removed from superstition. Epicurus' ideas have stood the test of time, and his view that death is nothing is increasingly accepted among those in the secular West. Yet many people have still not heard of his ideas, and the strength of the church means that religious dogmas continue to choke off anything that might undermine the fear surrounding death. The historic picture and the current world view could have been so very different; but religious power brokers saw no need for evidence-based thinking to get in their way.

Epicureans have long suffered at the hands of the church and their restrictive dogmas. For saying the mind died with the body, the followers of Jesus labelled Epicurus a heretic, which further suppressed his wider philosophical legacy. Remember that in Epicurus' lifetime there was no consensual view of religion to speak out against, and so there was no concept of heresy. It was only in the 2nd century CE that Epicurus was labelled a heretic, and a further 1600 years after his death when Dante's epic poem, *The Divine Comedy*, brought the heresy back to light. In modern parlance, Epicurus was air-brushed out of history. The clergy have a habit (no pun intended) of censoring ideas that are not 'on message', and during the medieval period almost all messages were controlled by the clergy as the main literate group. The ancient Greeks might have – disparagingly – called this Sophistry (the use of clever but false arguments with the intention of deceiving).

Reinterpretation of the truth by representatives of the church continues right into the modern era. Christopher Hitchens, one of the most high-profile atheists, was recently accused of having a death-bed conversion. Nick Cohen, writing in the Guardian in June 2016 noted:

the willingness of believers to go further and invent conversions where none existed satisfies their infantile need for fairy-tale endings. But when they recite falsehoods over the corpses of Paine, Darwin and now

Hitchens they move from the extremely seedy to the outright creepy: from vultures to vampires.

Thomas Paine wrote against the practices of the church over two hundred years ago, and at his death refused any audience with clerics. Darwin did not, as was widely reported, recant his evolutionary theory on his deathbed.

These comments on the fear of death require a little clarification. In a few months I will die, but for me, my family and friends, death is more than just that moment in time; there is the process of dying that comes before, and there is the time after my death where I leave an imprint. I was recently reviewing the excellent end of life guide for the Motor Neurone Disease Association, but the drafters of the document did not differentiate the fear of dying with the fear of death itself. It is important to separate the two and to understand the difference between them. I don't fear the process of my body becoming incapacitated, but I do have concerns that my care should not leave me too uncomfortable. Cory Taylor, in her book *Dying: A Memoir*, was writing as her physical condition deteriorated; she was initially 'frightened of dying' but over time became used to the idea, so much so that it became ordinary and unremarkable. In a truly philosophical turn, she noted of her fate, as she came close to death, that 'I will not miss dying'. The moment of death does not frighten me, because I now realise that my youthful fear of death was constructed by indoctrination which turned imagination into fear. Hell, damnation and torment have no basis in evidence and are sustained only through superstition. After I dismissed my youthful fears and accepted Epicurus' teachings that 'death is nothing', my life, and my impending death, got much easier.

2

Morality without god

Epicurus was able to present a philosophy of living a good life and having a good death without the need for god. Morality came before religious practises, and it will be around after religion is discarded: after all, H.L. Mencken wrote an essay back in 1922 listing at least 500 gods with no adherents. That's 500 dead gods. The important point here is that before religion interfered with morality, people were free to think about their lives and their world without the burden of superstition. As founding father Thomas Jefferson hoped, in his letter to John Adams, 'the human mind will someday get back to the freedom it enjoyed 2,000 years ago.'

Albert Camus suggested, in *The Rebel*, that philosophers and writers struggled without god, because, if god created everything, then without him morality and the world would just stop; there would be nothing left except immorality. This type of nihilism might make for good literature but it doesn't much help those who are facing death. Fortunately Bertrand Russell set out a raft of coherent arguments which non-believers facing death can draw strength from. His concluding remarks from *Why I am not a Christian* make the case well, and it resonates now as strongly as it did almost a hundred years ago.

> *The whole conception of God is a conception quite unworthy of free men... We ought to make the best we can of the world, and if it is not so good as we wish, after all it will still be better than what these others have made of it in all these ages. A good world needs knowledge, kindliness, and courage... It needs a fearless outlook and a free intelligence. It needs hope for the future, not looking back all the time towards a past that is dead, which we trust will be far surpassed by the future that our intelligence can create.*

This view, intelligent not superstitious, is a call for intellectual and social development, independent of religious morals.

The morality of religion was corrupted by the superstition of an afterlife which meant that people were fearful of death, but their lives were tainted as well. By decreeing people as sinful, their lives became a continual struggle to overcome sin, and although the words attributed to Jesus were not judgemental, his teachings were profoundly corrupted by the church's judgement on its followers. It seems reasonable to ask why sin took such a hold. The Belgian academic, Paul Verhaeghe, has explored this question in detail, and his book *What About Me?* gets close to answering how the church linked up with economic ideas to secure slavish compliance with their demands. By creating an afterlife and controlling access to it, people could be held accountable for their actions whilst alive. It is possible to substitute the words 'to ransom' for 'accountable' in that last sentence, since the church controlled the criteria for accessing the hereafter. Protestant capitalism increased the burden by further demanding a profit on earth as a credit for the afterlife, and mere sin was compounded into a judgement of both behaviour and productivity. The extraordinarily unchristian outcome of adding economics to twisted religion meant that poverty was interpreted as plain immorality, and it was easy for accusers to hand out blame in a chaotic, industrialising economy. The Calvinists went even further, agreeing human nature was flawed, but also demanding people's weaknesses be conquered, thus requiring individuals to achieve 'perfectibility' in their lifetimes. Laughably, the very idea of secularism was seen as failing god's tests, but they would say that, wouldn't they? Society, in part due to widespread illiteracy, accepted these burdens. The cruel interpretation of life – that people were sinful and inadequate until they proved otherwise – created much of the baggage that we drag along at the time of our death.

It's a tough job to break the stranglehold of religion when considering how to die well. The philosopher Antonio Gramsci described the intellectual and political superstructure that maintains dominant ideas as 'cultural hegemony', and the church's exceptional dominance gave them strong control. You might think it would be straightforward to proffer an alternative view, but dissent has not been tolerated. By way of an example, the group of intellectuals in pre-revolutionary France, the so-called *philosophes,* were openly non-believers within their small clique, but could not publish their work for fear of death. One of them, the Baron D'Holbach, wrote a detailed treatise, *The System of Nature*, dismissing the need for god in society, but he was forced to have the work published anonymously. The same held true in England, and until 1870 writers were required to give a surety of £800 against publishing anything considered blasphemous.

Cutting through both the judgementalism of the church and the economic overlay, the Scottish philosopher David Hume was at odds with both the puritans and the capitalists. Hume was an occasional visitor to the pre-revolutionary French intellectuals' dinners, and noted that economic demands were dependent on the all-encompassing pursuit of reason, which he thought wrong-headed. He argued that it should be our humanity that drives our behaviour, not an external system of control; neither a religious one, nor an economic one. Rather than controlling the emotions, the rational approach should be a servant to them; but like other good ideas that had come before, Hume's views did not gain traction against the church's cultural hegemony. What we now call neo-liberalism was allowed to override human emotions of empathy and friendship, and the pursuit of profit won out over our personal identity. The established church and the capitalists thus became odd bedfellows, as they undermined our well-being in their pursuit of power, and that partnership still operates up to the present time. This modern hegemony shifts perfectibility and the overcoming of sin as a problem for social or welfare reform and its narrow interpretation is a likely cause of much mental distress. It suits those in power to tweak the industrial revolution's moral values to fit global competitiveness because it's easy, but that doesn't make us more moral, more creative, more productive, or happier.

There is some good news. Darwin's theory of evolution has not been completely lost in the mix, but it's taken a long time to make inroads against a resistant establishment. The field of evolutionary psychology emerged fifty years ago, and reviewed the role of both individuals and groups, and although the initial ideas accepted a dominant role for individualism, the field has since sided with group selection, bringing community and kinship back into favour. Nowadays, evolutionary psychologists pronounce on many of the drivers influencing behaviour, but evolution is not, and never has been, about survival of the strongest, or those with the highest status. It is about survival of the fittest; those that are able to thrive under the prevailing conditions. Evolutionary ideas are therefore not about perfectibility, because survival depends on social and environmental factors that are subject to change. There cannot be one right solution. Because evolutionary theories have struggled to find their way into practical application, egotistical individualism still has the upper hand over social bonding. My view is that ideas about how to overcome flawed behaviour are themselves flawed. The neo-liberal economic requirements of 'measurable effectiveness' might be considered universal, but financial measurement is not a solution to replacing moral values, kinship and community, and it's not the answer to a good life, or a good death.

Of course, the views presented here could be described as just another belief, but it's belief based on evidence. A belief can be justified in one of two ways; it can be from a coherent set of ideas that underpin it, where all the evidence supports the bigger picture; or it can be a foundational justification, independent of other ideas. Religion is one such foundational belief, and that belief system argues that it does not require evidence. I don't deny that there are religious texts that might give comfort to some; but that's not the purpose of this book. I want to challenge the distorted morals pedalled by religion, and the fearful consequences that result for those facing death. I need a coherent set of ideas to give me comfort, and these are now available.

A strong argument that morals are independent of god was presented by Jonathan Haidt in his 2012 book *A Righteous Mind*. He established a coherent, independent set of moral values for modern society, and that's not as difficult as it sounds, because moral values existed before testaments or bibles. They came from simple, if primitive, practical guides, or if you like, an early version of health and safety, and these can be analysed and updated against sensible modern practices. Haidt was looking for universal morals, but suggests a word of caution here, because although the pattern of intellectual discussion from the ancient Greeks to the renaissance is widely adopted, and the history of Western philosophy is easily traced by all, it is still essentially a local European history. Haidt uses the acronym WEIRD to help set out how the West's ethical values developed, and it stands for: Western, Educated, Industrialised, Rich, & Democratic. Those living in such conditions are outliers, a minority against the population of the wider world, and being WEIRD is not itself a 'norm', although it probably is for readers of this book.

Haidt argues there are six moral foundations in the WEIRD population. These are:

- how we care for people and protect them from harm;
- how we approach liberty and oppression;
- how we deal with fairness and cheating;
- how we perceive loyalty and betrayal;
- how we perceive authority and subversion;
- how we manage our cleanliness, sanctity, and degradation.

Each of the six moral foundation forms a scale from one extreme to another. Take for example, the first pairing of care/protecting from harm: some people will focus more on providing care whilst others will focus on freedom from harm. The first takes a more communitarian view, the second is more libertarian, and although both have a common goal of protection, they have different means to that end; they are different sides of the same coin. It's the same for the other foundations (and if you want to explore this further, you can find more information at the Moralfoundations.org website).

What Haidt is trying to get across is how different religious and political groups end up in conflict about essentially the same outcomes. He identifies that liberals (the American term for those described as left leaning, or socialist in the UK) focus more on care and fairness, with an intention to make the world a fairer place, while Conservatives (they're called the same on both sides of the Atlantic) focus more equally on all six moral foundations, and temper fairness with a blend of liberty, loyalty and authority. Conservatives are already more comfortable with the traditional elements, and so they do not feel a need to strongly challenge the *status quo*. It is these foundations that should guide how we live and die, although the differences they generate cause conflict between the different political and religious groupings in WEIRD society.

The moral foundations for sanctity/degrading and fairness/cheating moral scales are found in many of the religious texts, because they relate to the safe operation of the largely tribal societies at that time, but the application of caring, liberty, loyalty and authority were developed later, and do not feature so heavily. When death occurred there was a need for cleanliness, to avoid disease, and to ensure a process of dealing with the bodies. Religions adopted in hot countries had specialists to deal with the dead, because there was a risk of spreading disease. Believers in India following Hinduism (meaning large body of water, or those who live beyond the Indus river) predated Judaism, so thousands of years ago in India there were separate groups for dealing with the dead. In Zoroastrianism (Zoroaster is the name of their alleged prophet), originating in Iran more than a thousand years BCE, those dealing with the dead even lived in separate communities, a kind of double protection. Modern Western religious practices have kept death at arm's length, but the pendulum is now swinging back with the increased life expectancy of the aging post-war baby boomers. A lot of terminal conditions are not well suited to dying in institutional medical centres, with their almost limitless medical interventions. People would prefer to die at home; and older people are fortunate to have lived long enough to get a terminal illness in their seventies, eighties or nineties. Bringing death back home means we need to manage death better within the family and our social groups, and a better understanding of the modern moral foundations is helpful to find a path through all the religious moral baggage about death.

Death in non-Western cultures has important differences. Followers of Islam (meaning surrender or submission), like followers of Jesus, believe in an afterlife, though the Jewish tradition focuses on earthly success and is less specific about it. The followers of Hinduism and Buddhism (meaning enlightenment) see their belief as more a set of philosophies than a religious creed; and they don't have the slavish requirements, or the judgemental approach. Death for them does not mean the end of being, because many sects believe in reincarnation. Other religions, such as those of ancestor worship see life as cyclical, where the dead move to a different place, even if it is not identified as heaven.

It is understandable that people might hope for a second chance because their first go was blighted by war, famine or disease, but there is no evidence of a re-run. Those who have no need of, or have total indifference to, religion can focus on living well, and dying well. For those wanting to die well without god there is a clear moral framework, independent of religion, and without the superstitious fear of hell and punishment in the afterlife. Because religious hegemony has worked its way so deeply into the fabric of our society that we are often unable to see a clear picture, and it determines our cultural choices. To help rebalance the scales against this, in the next chapter I offer a piece of symbolism as a counterweight against the imbalance.

3

Factism

Epicurus thought the gods did not concern themselves with human behaviour, but he still recognised them as immortal. At that time he may have been uncertain about their powers, or perhaps it was just politically astute for him to avoid outright denial, yet since his time there has been no hard evidence to support deity, and significant religious revelation is limited to just two instances in the last 3,000 years, Moses and Muhammed. Whilst you can believe those reports, if you want, they wholly lack evidence, and yet the machinery of religion has become established, institutionalised, buttressed by laws and customs and is part of our everyday language.

One simple example of how the scales are tipped in favour of religion is shown by the census that takes place in Great Britain every ten years. The last was in 2011, and among the questions, it asked 'What is your religion?' There was a choice of answers from six mainstream religions, as well as boxes for 'not religious', or 'other'. It does not matter that the question was voluntary, the issue at stake is the need to answer 'not religious' to the question 'What is your religion?' I am not religious, so the box titled 'Religion' was irrelevant to me. I didn't even want to consider it. The consequence of creating a bad question is people take the line of least resistance, so the 2011 census showed 61% of people in England and Wales as having a religious belief (53.48% Christian and 7.22% other), and 39% ticked 'No religion'. But when the Humanist Society asked a similar sample the different question, 'Are you religious?', only 29% said 'Yes' while 65% said 'No'. The census question was flawed, and it creates a false impression of religious support.

This is a situation caused by something called 'choice architecture', which was first written about in the 2009 book *Nudge* by Cass Sunstein and Richard Thaler. The choices available to us are dictated by the choice architecture we are offered. If you go into a fast food outlet you can choose between a burger or nuggets, or maybe a veggie option, and you can choose between tea, coffee or cola, but you don't have the choice of a rare roast beef Sunday lunch, or a nice bottle of red wine to go with it. You have choice, but not unlimited choice. The same is true for our culture. In the census I had the choice to say 'no religion', but that put the decision on me to opt out of religion. The cultural hegemony in WEIRD societies frames religion as the default position. There are many opt-out and opt-in decisions underlying the choices available in our culture, but they are framed as if belief in a religion is the accepted base line.

My stance is that if people want to believe in a god, they can have that choice, but they should choose to opt in to their belief; it's not my job to opt out. At the core it's about symbolism, and our culture is a product based upon symbols. There's been strong religious symbolism for a thousand years, during which time the church suppressed alternative symbols. As a result there is only weak symbolism for an absence of belief and so I propose a counterweight, and I call it *factism*.

The problem extends so far that it even undermines the choice of words we have for not being a believer. The word 'atheist' describes someone who does not believe, but it's taken from the perspective of a world of belief, so even this is pejorative. It's coined from a Greek root, but it's only been used from the renaissance, a time when religious devotion was culturally demanded, with no acceptable alternative. Atheism, literally meaning 'without gods', is an opt-out word *from* religion. In the same way the term 'non-believer' requires a break away from a religious belief system. There is limited choice, and few satisfactory words in our vocabulary to identify someone free of religion, so ensuring the available choice is biased towards believers. The word atheist is actually a misnomer, and it's the same for the term 'infidel', now loosely used as for all those outside Islamic belief, but its origins are from the followers of Jesus denouncing all the other religions. If someone is free of religion they do not see themselves as an atheist or an infidel; these are derogatory terms, not descriptive. I choose the term factist as a better symbol, a simple word that conveys guidance by facts rather than by superstition.

An agnostic is someone who believes that nothing is known, or can be known, of the existence or nature of god, and this could be seen as a safe bet. It gives only a weak analytical position, and it is still undermined by the cultural hegemony of religious doctrine. Such is the difficulty of escaping the clutches of religion that Camus, again in *The Rebel*, noted that even 'blasphemy is reverent, since every blasphemy is, ultimately, a participation in holiness.' Such a view may be rebellious, but it remains within the rules of the religious police. Factism is beyond religious rebellion as it does not recognise that rule book. I choose not to use or refer to the term god or Christ in conversation, or to use any lazy references to deity such as 'OMG' in texts. I have been able to retrain myself out of my youthful indoctrination, but it's not easy. None of these religious descriptions hold meaning for factists, except by way of peculiar social scientific analysis. Factists don't have to opt out of the believer's rules, or language, or give any recognition at all to the authority of religion. They merely see where religion is invoked as an agent for action, and then, without the need for superstition, take a factist position. Emphatically I am not a 'none' on a census form. Importantly too, I am not an atheist, agnostic, blasphemer, or infidel. I am none of these labels. In relation to a factist, the label of being irreligious should receive the same condemnation in Western society as abusive slang, like the old terms used to describe migrants from different cultural backgrounds; such terms are now considered unacceptable. Factists are slowly seeing how their choice architecture has been limited, and they are challenging and changing the options open to them. You might try it.

I've been asked how such a stance sits with a tolerance to religion, but it is not an intolerant position, and it does not challenge an individual's personal belief. Tolerance assumes that a person does not discriminate against another person's religious beliefs, even if they think that person's beliefs are wrong. A factist position identifies what plain language is appropriate for discussions, and what choices should be available without the usual built-in religious bias. It looks only to level the playing field against a cultural hegemony.

There are other labels for factists. Humanists would support a similar view, which is worthy, and they strongly challenge the role of the religion in education, but their values still operate within the choice architecture dominated by religion, In America they've coined the term 'Brights', in the hope that it will be seen as a hip or cult word; in the same way as 'gay' became cult for those in same-sex relationships, but I'm not sure if it will catch on. The pre- and post-revolutionary French intellectuals were called 'free thinkers', but it is not a popular or current description.

A denial of god helps dismantle the lazy use of terms associated with religion. The word evil (originally dislike or disapproval) has become a response against god's work, and I choose not to use it, because it camouflages the real roots of social disorder. Instead I look for more specific labels, and if people kill, steal or lie, calling it evil does not help identify solutions. There should be further and better analysis, and if the reasons for disorder were made plain, then better social progress could be made. This is the position taken by Russell in his speech *Why I am not a Christian*, mentioned earlier; apportioning blame on the basis of ungodly evil erodes our analytic ability, and our intelligence. The judgemental approach of the church, creating sin and immorality to serve its own ends, has meant tragic consequences for many, and the demands for perfectibility by Calvinists and neo-liberals has affected many more. You might think the population has been damned by both, but then the term damned isn't helpful for social understanding either; avoid it. Be alert too for surveys that suggest that religious believers cope better with grief and mourning. It is attendance at social events that is the critical factor, and having a good support network; the element of religion alone produces mixed empirical findings for coping, some better, and some worse. The general use of religious terminology sweeps away complex problems and makes us lazy thinkers, akin to the worst populism of the tabloid media. At a time when someone is facing death we need to think clearly about how we can help and, fortunately, much of the work has already been done for us. I draw on existing literature in part II to identify how to die well, and also to help those affected by loss and grief.

PART II –

PRACTICAL CONTRIBUTIONS TO A GOOD DEATH

4

The requirements for a good death

We've created systems in life to help us forget it won't last, to the extent that our lives are so busy we forget our human frailty, and we're offended by our fallibility. People from many different cultures now want more control over dying, but wanting control is not the same as getting it. Western specialisations, and the division of labour, have taken the management of death and dying away from families, and into the hands of institutions, much as Eastern religious specialists have long practised it. Now death is being brought back into the home.

The church says the only way to die well is through god, but as Chapter 2 has shown, morals came before religion, and reference to god is not a necessary requirement. Cory Taylor was stuck between the two, noting, 'One cannot face death without reflecting on questions of religious faith,' but she felt faith in god removed the opportunity for choice in a good death. Epicurus got closer to the heart of the matter by saying 'the art of living well and the art of dying well are one.' A good death is not something that just turns up at the end of life; it's something that needs to be considered all through life, but without the superstitious afterlife and its 'get out of jail free card' for past misdemeanours, and with no last minute apology to settle old scores. Preparation has to start much earlier. Bertrand Russell said we needed to live with knowledge, kindliness, courage and hope, and I think these are the starting essentials for a good death.

Discussion on various internet blogs describes a good death as being:

- Free from pain;
- Free from anxiety;
- Quick;
- Surrounded by family;
- Having all your affairs in order.

A checklist can be useful, but it is important to read between the lines too. A bereavement counselling friend tells me too many families have unresolved past grievances, and so suggests a dying person might need to question who they need to speak to, or think about who needs to speak to them. If matters are unreconciled then lives can end 'incomplete'. There is no time left to put these things off and yet, paradoxically, the way to get these matters aired is to give time and space for the topic to come out; and that means allowing silence to act as a trigger for dialogue, not just from the person dying, but from their family and friends too. There can still be time to open up on things left unsaid, and take a chance for closure before it's too late.

The website Mylastsong provides a different checklist to cover points of detail that people might not think of; it's particularly helpful to respect the wishes of the dying person who might not be aware they can articulate these issues:

- Tell me (what you want to be told about your terminal state);

- Treat me (what treatment you want, or want to refuse, when dying, and who should administer it);
- Take me (where you want to die);
- Please be there (who you want to be there);
- I want to see, hear, smell, feel, taste (a checklist of good things).

There's no need for reference to god in the checklists, and I was pleased to note there was none.

I have been told I am responding stoically to my disease, but that is to misunderstand stoicism. Stoicism promoted a deterministic world view of the universe, suggesting it has purpose, and that people should recognise the role of fate in any undertaking. Their reasoned analysis meant they chose not to react to adverse outcomes or disappointments. I am not deterministic, though I can choose to exert some control over my emotions, and that's easier with greater knowledge about my disease. I can't do much about it, but that doesn't mean I'm not emotional; I just haven't – so far – let my emotions take over. Instead I choose to engage even more with my friends, and continue to pursue learning.

The checklists overlook any incomplete discussions, and they can also overlook the need for a philosophical underpinning that comes from a deeper understanding of death. Epicurus said that death is nothing, but to get to that position he required an inner calmness to face his end. He called this state *ataraxia*, and although it's not a word in common usage today, it sums up the way I choose to approach my death. Ataraxia is described as the state of robust tranquillity, achieved when people have overcome belief in an afterlife. Like a good death, it's not something that can be taken off the shelf at the end of life; it needs to be built in to the living process as well. I was an Epicurean long before my diagnosis, so perhaps I was better prepared when that diagnosis came, and I think I'm better prepared as death gets nearer. Of course, I might just be kidding myself, and everyone else might have a far better coping mechanism, but I decided to take the thinking route through this problem. As Matt Damon says in the 2015 film, Martian, 'In the face of overwhelming odds, I am left with only one option; I'm going to have to science the shit out of this.' And that's partly why I wrote this book.

As well as telling us not to fear the gods, Epicurus sensibly advised his followers to surround themselves with trustworthy and affectionate friends, and the person dying should themselves be an affectionate and virtuous person worthy of trust. Writing as a man, I have to ask what it is about our culture that, when you say you have a terminal condition, the men start to hug you as the women have always hugged you. A diagnosis of a life-limiting disease might be considered inconvenient, but MND might be seen as more convenient than many other possibilities, as I've had time to spend with family, time to read, write and think. My disease is not painful, although the more difficult incapacity is yet to come. Importantly, I think I will have some control at the end, and I've been lucky to have lived so well, for so long. With forethought it's possible to reconnect any loose or lost social links, and it's possible to reconnect them without god. I know of some others who have died conveniently, particularly because they were very old. One sat down at the end of day, a cat in her lap, and just didn't wake up; another had a heart attack, after playing tennis, he just sat down on the bed and keeled over. Well, I think they died conveniently, but they aren't here to confirm or deny whether it was a good death, and they may have disagreed.

Different people will have different priorities for their checklists, and you'll have to make your own mind up about how to die well. Ruth Picardie wrote, in *Before I say Goodbye*: 'Great! I'm going to die of cancer, but I'm going to go bonkers first,' but her husband described those comments as bravado. She went on to develop an 'A list' of those who failed the cancer victim test for being unable to empathise with her. These people, she said, were to be banned from her funeral. She was trying to get a handle on something when almost all other controls were out of whack. She wanted people to recognise her situation and relate to it, and I can understand her need for such a list. When time is short it is not to be wasted on stuff that's going against the grain. The absurdity of redundant social conventions, social niceties, or playing games about pecking order, is starkly magnified by death's proximity. I choose to pursue Epicurus' ataraxia as my condition deteriorates, and I hope many more people will come to understand ataraxia as a common approach to dying. I've got my affairs in order and emphatically I do not fear death, because I am an Epicurean; I believe I will have a singularly good death.

5

Language and behaviour

Communication can get complicated. An American student, Andrew Osborne, commented on *Ars moriendi*, noting 'the depths of a language provoke very real (albeit incommunicable) emotions associated with the loss of a loved one', and this begs the question: 'What is it about death that is incommunicable?' You may have experienced situations where there is an uncomfortable silence when the conversation turns to dying; it is not uncommon. Some may have 'off pat' or well-rehearsed comments to offer, and I don't doubt their sincerity, but many people, whether they have faith or not, are just dumbfounded, and some go into denial. Yet there are helpful and constructive ways to engage in discussion about death and dying.

Each of the many different players that need to have conversations will have a different set of requirements. Some are dying, others suffering grief; some will fear death, and will others worry about care. So many permutations makes engaging in effective communication difficult. Some people will have heightened sensitivity, while some just can't find the right words; others will be direct and open and will tell you straight, and others pause or hesitate before offering a view;

some focus on business matters, others on their emotions. My own search for literature to help me better understand dying, started with John Banville's *The Sea*, because the reviews credited it with a good description of mourning a partner's death. The narrator's first response to his wife's terminal diagnosis is described as embarrassment, and he did not know what to say, where to look, or how to behave. He used the term 'dissembling' of his own behaviour, in the sense of concealing or disguising his true feelings or beliefs. It suggests a lack of capacity to be open about someone having a terminal condition, and the novel's plot was further complicated by his wife not wanting to tell anyone, even their daughter, until close to death.

I find myself asking why dying should be embarrassing, because everyone's going to die at some time; Banville's ability to describe embarrassment as a response is a useful starting point and his insight gave me a chance to explore the behaviours and languages we use. Responses of shock and embarrassment to someone dying reflect a lack of preparedness for such news, yet it seems illogical to think it should be remote from our practical social experience. Taylor draws out the themes of embarrassment and misery that were also identified by CS Lewis in his book *A Grief Observed*. Lewis hated people who clumsily tried to bridge across into his grief, and he hated them if they didn't try.

The essentials to talking about death and dying are to seek the right time and the right place, to ask questions and listen, to be honest, and to get help. The UK Dying Matters coalition is a good place to start, and they have a very helpful website. To say communication is time-critical would be stating the obvious; if time is short, conversations need to be more direct. This chapter considers what we know and can say, what works and what doesn't, and what seems to be beyond our language capacity.

Behaviour and language to news of death is culturally dependent and we know it is still disproportionately influenced by religious institutions. Institutions are self-perpetuating bodies; they're conservative, and they work to promote the needs of the institution, but not necessarily the needs of the clients. The technical term for this is *autopoietic*, and in plain English it means they are looking after their own interests first. The consequence, for those institutions working with the management of death, is that they are behind the curve in adapting their approach to the current needs of clients. Many are resistant to change; they have invested heavily in old knowledge and old practises and they're more dependent on old routines than listening to their client's needs. Religion is dependent on ancient superstitions, independent of any evidence, so it is not surprising that a common complaint against Western funerals is they are more about god than the person who's died. In the same way some clinicians, funeral directors and celebrants at funerals cling to their traditional methods based on an out-of-date world view of their roles and function.

Taylor spoke of an aversion to discussing death and, for me, this was reinforced in 2016, when I attended the launch of NICE (National Institute for Clinical Excellence) guidelines for the care of those with Motor Neurone Disease. The guidelines were generally well drafted, but included a long section on the withdrawal of non-invasive ventilation. What that section failed to indicate was the consequence of withdrawing that ventilation; it meant the patient died. Instead the report found the more circuitous language of clinical terminology more comfortable, such as 'avoiding untimely case closure'. What it didn't say was that untimely case closure meant the patient died. An aversion to discussing death in clinical management makes it even more difficult for families and friends to comprehend what's going on. If a clinical linguistic style undermines sensitive patient emotions, then professionals need to have even better communication skills to be able to help others.

There are some basic ground rules with common acceptance around the language of dying, though culturally the English aren't good at it. I recall the first time I heard the phrase 'Sorry for your loss', in the television police series, *NYPD Blue*, as detective Sipowicz consoled a relative of a murder victim. It's not very English, though it's common in Ireland, and it's more effective than most English language phrases used over the years. In similar vein, a recent photo of a poster at a bereaved American family home went viral on social media. It said:

> *"Guidelines (rules): Hugs encouraged (except for the bear); Fond memories appreciated; Laughter welcomed*
>
> *We kindly ask you to refrain from saying; He is in a better place; It's part of a bigger plan (anything about plans); At least…"*

These people are spelling out how to pass the Picardie test. A friend recently stopped by and welcomed me with the sentence 'I'm really sorry to hear about your diagnosis'. She was direct, open, and straight away had the intention to build a strong social connection.

Responses traditionally bedded in religion undermine our ability to think about real empathy. We've given up responsibility for managing our responses, and given it to the vicar. Here's one example from the internet:

Definitely make sure they know Jesus if they want to live forever in heaven. I'm sure you'll want to see your friend again on the other side, and Jesus is the only way into heaven.

This says nothing about the person dying, and nothing about their immediate needs. If someone said anything like this to me, they'd go straight to Picardie's A list, and be barred from my funeral. That's their belief, not mine, and they're making no effort to talk to me.

There is no single formula for getting it right, it takes effort. 'Sorry for your loss' is good in some places, but just a cliché in others. 'How are you doing?' is said to be effective on some websites, but shunned as negative by others. If you ask that question you have to be prepared for listening to a detailed answer, and then be prepared to help; otherwise don't ask. There is common ground on the following points as being positive contributions:

- Do something or say something. Doing nothing is not an option.
- Agree that they will be sorely missed.
- Ask what you can do to help specifically, avoid non-committal generalities.
- Care about the grievers, tell them they are in your thoughts, and send them your love.
- Work on the relationship with whoever is suffering. Don't deny or underestimate their grief.

You don't know, and can't know, how they are feeling, so don't say so! Don't tell them you're always at the end of phone, we all are! There are no rational consolations for the emotional state grievers are in; let them grieve. If you go visiting, then be clear why you are going. Callanan and Kelly, in their book *Final Gifts: Understanding and Helping the Dying*, note that many dying people are lonely, because they are visited by friends who talk idly about the weather or sport. Such chatter keeps the dying person from talking intimately about what's really happening to them. If you feel you should visit because it is expected of you, double check your expectations. Make sure there's a purpose.

People facing death focus intently on the language used, because it may be one of the few things they can do in their final days; some language is not appropriate. According to Atul Gawande in his book *Being Mortal*, palliative care workers focus on what can be done, not what's in the past. They say 'I wish things were different' rather than 'I'm sorry things turned out this way'. It's a subtle shift that removes the risk of introducing guilt, or tripping over historic baggage. It avoids the negatives of lost capacity, and focuses on the remaining capability, or what is possible. This approach sidesteps discussion about any disability, or its cause. For the same reasons they say 'how are you today?' with the emphasis on today, the here and now. Such simple advice is helpful. Gawande is also right up to date with what's important, covering such topics as letting go, and discussing the fine line between medical intervention and when to say no. In their 2009 British Medical Journal article *Performing the good death: the medieval Ars moriendi and contemporary doctors*, Kevin Thornton and Christine Phillips argue that medical institutions continue to construct death as a battle against physical debility, even when patients may have different wants for their deaths. Clinicians tend to look for technical or chemical interventions, whereas palliative care workers look to help people overcome their anxieties. Medical intervention may delay the inevitable, but it could also cause additional suffering.

We've inherited a culture with an underlying expectation of fairness; indeed, it's one of Haidt's six moral foundations, and perhaps our expectation comes from parents wanting to protect their children. But life isn't fair, and it never has been. Westerners are lucky to have seen extraordinary increases in life expectancy in their lifetimes, but that doesn't make life fair. To ask the question: 'why me?' is unfortunately to ask the wrong question. Harsh but true. It's historic, it won't fix anything, and it doesn't work. From time to time, Taylor asked the 'why me?' question, even though she knew it was dumb to ask and she realised a practical focus on the future still allowed for caring, and for fond memories to be shared.

One training workshop for those working with the dying listed the following phrases: at peace; at rest; in heaven; lost; in a better place; asleep; and gone away. In the same way the writers of obituaries have options that include death as gain (a better place), death as loss (gone away), and death as a metaphor (at rest), and again, none of these work for me. Dying creates loss, but people are not lost – they're dying, they're not tired of life – they're dead. They only rest in peace because their whole life was framed by the church's teachings as being an inadequate, failed sinner forced into a perpetual struggle. Whose fault is that? The language in Monty Python's parrot sketch tries to cover all the bases as it trails out a classic list of English euphemisms; rest in peace, kicked the bucket, shuffled off his mortal coil, joined the choir invisible, but it clearly nails it in the opening statement: 'This parrot is dead.' The trouble with WEIRD communities, and that would pretty well encompass all Monty Python fans, is that we're not readily familiar with the plain English equivalent of death and dying, and we don't think hard enough about it.

My own approach has been to embrace the subject as an academic exercise, although I acknowledge that some family and friends may have found this morbid interest distracting and unhelpful. The dying person is likely to be dependent on those around them for support, and at the same time those supporters need help from friends and family, and even from the dying person. Problems arise when language is at cross purposes. Simple misunderstandings can easily escalate to dislocate social bonds and behaviours. Topics can be introduced too early, or too late, and the more you think about it, the more you fluff your lines. If you focus too much on what you're trying to say, you won't pick up the clues and cues in the conversation; don't try to change yourself, you can't do that. Make it your task to bridge possible isolation, make it a dialogue with a proper two-sided conversation (where capabilities allow) and avoid monologues. Listen, and if you can't find the words, try touch as an alternative. Over dinner last week my daughter ended a conversation with, 'So says the man seeking empathy as he withers away to an early death.' I looked at her sideways as she added, 'Too soon?' And we all burst out laughing.

I'm not in a rage, and I'm not fighting my disease. What's the point in that? There are common pleas that people 'fight' their cancers or illnesses, and obituaries frequently say someone has 'lost their battle' with their disease. Dr Kate Granger, famous for her "My name is" campaign, died of cancer in 2016, but she also spoke out against cancer being a battle; she was concerned that if you die you get labelled a loser. So I'm no fan of Dylan Thomas' poem where he says:

> *Do not go gentle into that good night,*
> *Old age should burn and rave at close of day;*
> *Rage, rage against the dying of the light.*

Instead I'd be much happier with Roger McGough's idea that it would be convenient if, in old age he was:

> *mown down at dawn, by a bright red sports car*
> *on my way home, from an all-night party*

The good news about preparing yourself for discussions about death and dying is that you have tools at your disposal you might not be aware of. We all have something called tacit knowledge, it's that ability to know more than you can say, and there are behaviours and mannerisms that we automatically employ even if we don't immediately recognise them; things like holding eye contact, being tactile, making a shift in intonation. If you examine these, you might become more aware of how you are adapting your behaviour; you're stretching yourself to engage compassionately, but doing it without conscious awareness. Explicit knowledge is what we learn in formal exchanges of language, and this chapter explicitly gives a few tips, but tacit knowledge is personal and it comes out only in specific situations. It's like the stuff that Andrew Osborne said was 'incommunicable'. As with the alternative ground rules noted above, you might not be able to find the words, but: hugs encouraged, memories and laughter welcome. If you have the right intention it's not hard to make that bridge, even if the words don't come. Get rid of your baggage and engage. People need clear communication to know if they're having a 'good death'.

6

Loss

My local vicar (and good friend) recently challenged my lack of belief by saying that Epicureanism lacked compassion. She might be right, but things need to be put into context. Epicurus' belief system was founded at the time when Greece faced problems of war, death and famine on a frequent, even daily, basis. Such threats were real, and closer to home than for our modern Western society. Modern healthcare, and our analytical approach to risk assessment, means death is a less common occurrence than for the ancient Greeks because institutional systems make it a remote experience. We have a quite different response to loss than would have been the case for the Greeks. If Epicureanism does not translate so well to our cosseted Western societies, it is worth exploring what modern culture means when we talk of loss.

Being better educated and leading busier lives should perhaps help us cope better with the death of a loved one, but the impact of loss is poorly understood. Daniel Kahneman and Amos Tversky were awarded the Nobel Prize for Economics in 2002, for their Prospect Theory of economics. They showed that earlier economic theories posing 'rational man' as balancing out gains and losses of equal value was not the case. Rather than rational, our human response to loss is anything but. It is twice as powerful a motivator as an equivalent, non-emotional, potential gain, so it hits us harder than we think: twice as hard. That's only for financial loss, so it might be even more significant for complex emotional losses, and should not to be dismissed lightly. We need to re-evaluate our expectations when facing death or giving support to the dying, in the light of this knowledge.

Elisabeth Kübler-Ross' 1960s book *On Death and Dying* was a pioneering text to address how society and the medical profession might tackle the subject, and her work was instrumental in the development of palliative care. It's dated now and contains all the weaknesses of paternalism, inequality and insensitivity that would not be acceptable in a 21st-century text, and importantly it goes through a series of chapters as if there are stages to loss and grief, including; denial, anger, bargaining, depression, and finally acceptance. These have been interpreted as being the requirements for managing loss, but different people have different needs, and Kübler-Ross is now on record agreeing that her book has been misinterpreted. It was of its time, and it stimulated much better analysis in the books that followed. The MND Association's *End of Life* guide helpfully uses the phrase 'anticipatory grief' for the expectation of losing someone close before they actually die. For terminal illnesses the grieving process starts before death, and that should not be underestimated. Anticipatory grief is part of anticipatory mourning, and people may feel any of the so-called 'stages' identified by Kübler-Ross. Shock and dismay would be common, and they may struggle with a degree of helplessness in the face of the life changes before them. Simple tasks can become complicated, and it's energy sapping to compensate. Those grieving whilst caring also need support and time to adjust. It's hard.

W H Auden's poem *Funeral Blues* (Stop all the clocks...) helpfully gives a little insight into the magnitude of loss, and Joan Didion's *The Year of Magical Thinking* spells out the physical symptoms of loss identified in an early study. This includes sensations occurring in waves lasting from twenty minutes to an hour, including choking, shortness of breath and an empty feeling. She went on to say that grief was passive, but mourning (that is, dealing with the grief) needed attention.

Current thinking now posits four identifiable elements to loss and grieving, but these are not stages, and there is no requirement to follow a sequential pattern. The elements are:

- Numbness-disbelief,
- Separation distress;
- Depression/mourning;
- Recovery.

Separation distress can include a seeking and a yearning. Occasionally it becomes complicated (or complex) grieving where recovery is delayed, or the griever gets stuck in one or more of the distressing stages. Roland Barthes' *Mourning Diary* tells of his difficulty in coming to terms with his mother's death. He goes to pieces, saying the term mourning is too psychoanalytic; he is plain suffering. His commentary is neither uplifting, nor analytical, but it is a testament to the power of grief after loss. Both Barthes and Didion were great writers, intelligent and privileged people, and they struggled to function at even a basic level, either to manage the home or work. They both displayed considerable physical symptoms, practical difficulties and emotional distress.

The power of loss to affect people's well-being means it's important to be compassionate. Compassion is defined as 'to hold a concern for the sufferings or misfortunes of others'. But being an Epicurean does not mean I have lost compassion; indeed, Epicurus himself was compassionate in bequeathing his belongings to his friends, and for giving helpful advice on the topic of death and dying. I consider an Epicurean life and a factist death no less compassionate than one associated with religion. There is no lack of compassion where people are loving, asking, listening, talking, hugging and just being friends. Compassion requires the intent to build a strong social bond, and god is irrelevant to that discussion. If my vicar thought Epicurus was not compassionate, a re-reading of Kübler-Ross shows how people's expectations have shifted; it suggests she expected the dying, and their grieving friends and family, to sort out their feelings about guilt, responsibility and rejection in time for any forthcoming death. With professional advice like that it is perversely pleasing to note that she was worried not everyone could afford counselling. Perhaps it was just as well.

Picardie says those who believe they are going to die tend to die sooner, and that living without hope is miserable. Hope needs to be seen in a shorter timeframe, and so it is important your intentions shine through in your language and behaviour to support someone who is dying, or for others facing loss. Be a friend; do something useful.

7

Assisted suicide v palliative care

As the baby boomers move into their seventies, they'll want as much control as possible to ensure they have good deaths. I vividly recall many years ago, when my mother was close to the end of her life and wasting away, we asked what procedure had been performed after an operation and she said, 'I don't know, I didn't want to bother them!' It's a generational thing, and I don't blame my mother for her submissive approach, but for my own death I want to be in the metaphorical driving seat. I guess many of the baby boomers feel the same way.

Chapter 2 proposed there is a strong moral framework without god, we have no need to fear death, and it is now possible to consider how best to end life within a modern code without the distorting interference of religious superstition. The late Lord Rix is a prime example of the need to make sensible decisions on this issue. A longstanding champion of rights for people with disability, he decried assisted suicide as a danger to that group until he was, himself, diagnosed with a terminal illness, and then he wanted urgent legislation to give him the right to assisted death. It might be judged as being hypocritical, but let's look at the issues and the arguments for and against.

Definitions here are important, to avoid some of the problems of miscommunication that we've already touched upon.

- Euthanasia is intentionally ending a life in order to relieve pain and suffering, and it's voluntary euthanasia if the patient is in control.
- Assisted suicide is the suicide of a patient suffering from an incurable disease, taking lethal drugs provided by a doctor for that purpose. This almost exactly overlaps with the definition of voluntary euthanasia.
- Assisted dying allows the terminally ill person to have a choice over the manner and timing of their imminent death.

Different campaigns use specific terms to support their positions or to twist them pejoratively for opposing a view. Those in favour of assisted suicide will call it assisted dying, or dying with dignity, whilst those opposed will focus on the term suicide or euthanasia, casually dropping the term voluntary off their press releases. Importantly, assisted suicide enables someone who is not actually dying to choose death over life.

Both assisted suicide and euthanasia are legal in Belgium, Luxembourg, the Netherlands, and, from June 2016, Canada. In these countries a doctor is allowed to administer medication directly to the patient. Switzerland allows circumstances where no offence is committed by the act of helping someone to die, but they must self-medicate. In the US, the states of Washington, Oregon, and Vermont allow assisted suicide, and, again, in June 2016, physician assisted suicide became law in California. The Assisted Dying Bill in the UK, in 2015, followed the US state of Oregon's model, where terminally ill adults who meet strict upfront criteria and satisfy legal safeguards, have the option to take life-ending medication and die peacefully at home.

The UK-based organisation Care Not Killing has links to faith-based groups, and it's no surprise that the 26 bishops in the House of Lords voted against the UK Bill in 2015. This is an example of institutional conservatism; it's not people who are influencing the vote, it's the institutional position that has the most influence. The *raison d'etre* is to vote against change that undermines the primary purpose of the institution, and many attempts to introduce such legislation fall specifically because of the religious lobby. That's not to say that everyone against assisted suicide is pro-religious, but a common idea put forward against euthanasia and assisted suicide by religious institutions is that life is sacred, and therefore life is always better than death. This is rejected by many, particularly those facing a painful death, but the moral barrier presented by religious groups remains based on superstition.

If assisted dying is not available, as in the UK, then the option is either a trip to a country that allows it, or palliative care. Palliative care gives patients the necessary care, and pain relief, to make them comfortable, and it offers support to the dying person's family. Hospice care is not necessarily institutional, and the majority of the hospice movement's work is in people's own homes.

The concept of 'quality of life' is an important aspect of the ethical argument, and the organisation Dignity in Dying argues that those close to death should have choice over where they die, and have expert information on their options. Dignity means worthy of respect, but it is the life that defines the person, not their death. It is entirely a matter of perception whether someone's situation at the end of life provides dignity or not. Surely, the act of requiring care is separate from an assessment of dignity. If people perceive being terminally ill, losing weight, and being incontinent as losing dignity, then this is culturally determined, and our perceptions are wrong. This should be challenged, because being worthy of respect at the time of death is not the same as having autonomy (control). It's about symbolism again, but 'autonomy in dying' isn't alliterative or poetic.

There is some blurring of the processes at work here. A few years ago, many of the practises used in end of life care were considered to be euthanasia in all but name, but further reviews have tried to put a clear line between the two. Taylor, dying in Australia, knew she could not legally access any help for assisted suicide, so she bought drugs over the internet that would end her life. She didn't use them, but took comfort from having them. In the UK in 2016, Simon Bonner, dying of MND, chose to go public with his assisted dying in Switzerland, and to make it a TV documentary. After watching it, I considered that assisted dying was a pretty cold and clinical process, and that palliative care would provide me with sufficient control at the end. Of course, I'm still to test that.

The decision to consider assisted dying is another problem where there is limited choice available. It is illegal in the UK to help someone kill themselves, and so the scope for a conversation about assisted dying is limited to an either/ or debate; either palliative care or travel abroad. Introducing the topic for discussion is constrained by the practicalities of the legal framework, because the act of assisting is presented as morally wrong, but in what way are the people of Belgium, California, Canada, the Netherlands or Luxembourg so very deviant from the moral values of the British?

It was because of such a limited 'either/or' choice that I had to think harder about my options. My initial decision defaulted to palliative care, because I did not want a foreign trip to an austere clinical setting (well, the one I saw looked pretty bleak); it would not have been conducive to helping my family come to terms with my death. Given a wider choice I would opt for assisted dying at home, at a point when I could no longer effectively function. But this creates another decision point for the choices available. People with cancer may still have mobility when close to death, but people with MND may lose all capacity for the mobility that enables them to self-administer the fatal drugs. Does self-administration have to be part of the legalisation? It seems arbitrarily daft to exclude help from doctors when they will be in attendance. If I was no longer conscious, having already agreed to refuse water and food, my death would be inevitable; just a matter of time, and living longer would be an unnecessary period of stress, and a burden for my family. I want the option to live well while I can, and, after the brain has ceased to communicate with the outside world, I would want to die quickly and not wait for the body to fail over coming days or weeks. Whether or not I am in pain, a period of unconsciousness could be uncomfortable, so, subject to whatever criteria is built into any safeguards and written into my advance decisions, my death should come sooner rather than later. I should not need to contribute further for the act to follow.

Atul Gawande wrote about letting go in his book *Being Mortal*. The issue for me is to spell out how I interpret the Gawande Test, so that my family and the medical (hospice) team understand my wishes. The decision for me will rest on the following criteria:

- Level of pain/discomfort;
- Ability to function to my satisfaction.

At no point should the cost of care become a consideration, nor should perceptions about dignity come into play. My expectation, as I near end of life, is that I will be unable to speak, unable to move, unable to eat or to swallow, and my breathing will be difficult. It goes without saying, given those circumstances, that I will not be able to care for myself, dress myself, eat, or go to the toilet, and I expect to be confined to bed. So when does the benefit of nutritional support outweigh the costs to the patient? The patient, family members, and healthcare providers need to discuss and agree upon the goals of nutritional support during palliative and hospice care. While there is now a heightened awareness of respecting the 'patient's' wishes, I remain of the view that, as someone dying, I am not strictly a patient.

The 'good' news' for me is that the losses for each failing element of my body, my legs, arms, swallowing, and breathing, are co-terminus. They will all fail at the same time, so the decision to stop food, water and breathing assistance will therefore be easier. I do not want a tracheostomy, and nor do I want constant pain. Water deprivation increases the body's production of endogenous opiates; they create a euphoric state that has been associated with a reduction in pain. Non-invasive ventilation is supportive, not curative, and it is primarily to assist while other problems are managed. For my condition there is therefore a strong argument that non-invasive ventilation will only make a contribution for a short period of time, though this is not the case for the more common types of MND, where longevity is much greater and ventilation is a significant contribution to life expectancy. I am aware of the consequences of such a decision. I will likely die sooner.

With palliative care, the MND Association provide a 'Just in Case' box for the emergency treatment of acute respiratory distress that occurs in the terminal stage. Subject to GP approval, it might include the drugs diazepam (anti-anxiety), diamorphine (heroin for pain relief), chlorpromazine (for the effects of the heroin), and hyoscine (for sickness). I've got mine ready for when I need it. It might be the first, and last, time I get stoned, but I probably won't remember it, and won't be able to tell anyone about it..

There is comforting data for me from the medical journals. One report, from Neudart et al, noted:

The data show that most MND/ALS patients (Germany 88%, UK 98%) died peacefully, and no patient 'choked to death'. Around half (G 55%, UK 52%) of the patients died at home. The main palliative measures in place during the terminal phase were... morphine (G 27%, UK 82%) and benzodiazepines (G 32%, UK 64%). The use of these palliative measures was judged to be beneficial by almost all relatives.

If I am right, I won't know much about my death. If I am wrong I will have a week or two of discomfort. I'm getting close the go/no go decision for the option to refuse food, water and ventilation. My arms have stopped working and they cause me pain, I am fed a liquid diet through a tube because I risk of getting food in my lungs, talking is very difficult, I can't keep my head up, and so far, everything is predictable. A dying friend said they weren't being brave, because bravery suggested they had some kind of choice. For me, I think the characters from the wizard of Oz, the people in need a heart, a brain and courage are the UK legislators. I think those facing end of life deserve a better choice.

8

Decommissioning

Following my diagnosis there was much to do. I hold a Master's degree in Project Management, so that was my approach to dying; just another part of a project plan. The last phase of any project is decommissioning, so here is my to-do list.

Task 1: Who to tell. My wife and I agreed to tell our children (then 28 and 24 years old) straightaway. We also told close friends. Our family needed support and understanding from a wider group, and we got it.

Task 2: Know your disease. I'm a researcher, and I needed to know what I had to help me cope. That decision moved me from victim to an active role, and I loved it. It gave me motivation and interest, and opened up a much needed area of productivity to replace the commercial work I was not able to do. As Burnap said back in 1848, 'The three grand essentials of happiness are: Something to do, someone to love, and something to hope for.' Study of my condition fulfilled the first essential; the second was already in place; and the last, well that needed redefining into a shorter time frame. My first projection was that I would die within eighteen months, and I now think I'm stretching that out by a few weeks. Significantly, there were few medical decisions I had to make. There were no agonising choices about having or refusing surgery or other treatments. There was one possible drug (Rilutek), but the effects were marginal, and it made me feel rough, so I stopped taking it. The disease will take its course, a linear degradation to death.

Task 3: Write a will. Our wills had recently been updated so there was no action required.

Task 4: Power of Attorney. Power of attorney (POA) for someone with a terminal disease requires two elements; finance and medical. The first gives power for controlling my money, but my wife and I have had a joint account for 35 years, so it required a legal adjustment, not a change in our relationship. The second element gave my wife power for my medical care and supervision (see also Task 6: Advanced decision below). The POA was completed in the first few months after diagnosis, and though it's not cheap (£1,000), it should save problems later.

Task 5: Succession planning. I worked freelance, but even before the diagnosis I had to cancel work because I was not able to speak clearly. Years earlier I'd had conversations with my clients about the risk of me falling under a proverbial bus, and we had long planned for that day when I would not be able to help. It was easy to arrange succession planning and pass the work over to other people. I quit all my committees (lots of them) though for some we had to recruit other committee members or trustees before I could resign.

Task 6: Advanced decision. I drafted this within six months of diagnosis and gave it to my neurologist and GP. It's a general statement of Do Not Resuscitate (properly called an Advance Decision to Refuse Treatment, under the Mental Capacity Act 2005). I reserve the right to refuse water, food and ventilation, in an effort to hasten my death. I could be kept alive longer if they gave me a tracheostomy and fed me intravenously, but that appears to be an uncomfortable situation to be in, and I see no purpose in continuing to live in that state. There is no moral requirement for it. This decision overrides the delegated power of attorney noted in task 4. If I am unable to communicate with speech or hand signals, I will make the letter 'Z' (the last letter of the alphabet) with my eyes, and then my family know I am ready to be left to die.

6A: Preparations prior to death. Recognising that my advanced decision specifies not having certain medical interventions, there were a couple of things I wanted to do to make things easier. The first was to have a feeding tube put in, should my swallowing pack up while the rest of me was still good. Patients with MND are at a higher risk of getting food stuck in their lungs (aspiration), and it seemed daft to waste away if everything else was working. I had a PEG feeding tube fitted six months after diagnosis, and was fortunate not to need it for a further ten months. I also put my voice into a (free) computer programme so that if I could not speak I could type words into my computer to talk to my family and friends with my own voice, not a manufactured (American) one. With both these things, whether you need them immediately, or not, it's better to do them early.

Task 7: Finances. This was not a big deal for us, and I guess that's the same for many others, but we met with our independent financial adviser, who made some helpful suggestions about pensions. We were able to clear the mortgage after 34 years, and I'll leave some money for the hospice.

Task 8: Bills. I managed all the bills and we did not want to wait until after I died to transfer the responsibility. We agreed for my wife to set up a new account, in her name only, and we transferred all the major bills to that account.

Task 9: Funeral arrangements. I sorted this early. Six months after diagnosis I met with the funeral director and chose a nice, sustainably resourced coffin made out of sea grass. I met with a humanist celebrant who agreed to officiate, and I paid for everything up front.

Task 10: Driving. I told my insurers and the DVLA three months after the diagnosis, but continued to drive for another nine months before deciding to stop, when my body was still working pretty well.

Task 11: Welfare benefits. Three months after diagnosis I was told of my entitlement to a Personal Independence Payment. I couldn't work and it was helpful. The paperwork was done very quickly, with one phone call, and it was all was agreed within a week.

Task 12: Property management. That was my key domestic role, and a general effort was quickly made to get the house into good order. All those jobs that I'd been putting off were completed (fencing, decorating, dodgy door handles etc.)

whilst I was still capable of doing them. We cleared out the attic and sheds of old stuff that might have been nostalgic, but it mostly wasn't. Contractors were hired for window cleaning and gardening when I could no longer do that work.

Task 13: Bucket list. I didn't have a bucket list. I've tried to be a Green activist, but I've still consumed too much of the Earth's precious resources. I've been part of the problem, not part of the solution. The planet can't cope with everyone jetting around to see foreign sites, just because they can, and so the idea of a bucket list did not appeal to me. I was asked to do two things on my wife's bucket list, and we agreed to see Paris ('*We'll always have Paris*') and the Fjords. I'd liked to have walked more of the Welsh and Scottish highlands, but someone else can do that for me. I live in a nice house in a beautiful place, and that's better than hot beaches, jungles or exciting cities; it's home. I read great books instead, and I buy most of them second hand.

Task 14: Project learning. You could write a book to explain what you've learned about dying, or you could write a book that explains what you've learned in life. The learning should be captured for others' benefit. There's a data stick and laptop for the family with all the files, records, warranties, maintenance plans, gardening tips, and contact details.

Task 15: Celebrate success. Keep loving. Remember the good times, the good things, and the good work done. Remember family and friends, events (mostly parties), and the love shared. There's a thank-you letter for those closest to me, to be read after I'm dead. Remember the best bits often. Raise a glass to me occasionally.

A word of caution is required here, and that is, don't write things off too early. Receiving a terminal diagnosis isn't much fun, and there's an immediate emotional response of distress, grief and fear, but that intense feeling passes, given time, and it's then replaced by a complex set of emotional responses triggered by day–to-day events. I don't think it's a roller coaster, that's far too dramatic a description for me, although for some people feeling out of control will make it seem a realistic picture. It's certainly fluid, and that's what makes it worth looking at in more detail.

From the date of my diagnosis I kept a diary to record my physical capabilities and general feelings about how life was changing. A number of patterns emerged that were unexpected. One of these patterns was something called reflexivity – a social theory defined as being a circular relationship between cause and effect. To some degree this is already illustrated in Chapter Three, where the choices available to people for voting about their religious beliefs affects whether or not they actually say they have a belief. When someone scrutinises an action they find it bends back on, or otherwise affects, the person instigating the action, so people are already thinking they should have a belief before they answer the question. My own recent research into the teaching of creativity showed that if subjects were asked if they taught people how to be creative they mostly said yes, but if I asked them for examples of what they delivered in terms of teaching creativity, they mostly said they hadn't thought about it. In social research, asking a question of a research subject can trigger ideas in the subject's mind that gives their response a bias. For people with a terminal diagnosis this reflexive response occurs in a least two situations or categories; contact with clinicians and assessing personal loss of capacity.

In the first situation, I perceive contact with clinicians as almost always a negative experience. After the initial impact of a terminal diagnosis, people look to get on with their lives as best possible, and on any given day they will still plan for the future, and live in the moment. Their responses will include both positive and negative emotions, but most people will look to optimise positive experiences. However, the simple process of getting through the week will require contact with the services that will sustain them through their period of decline; services such as doctors, nurses, specialist advisers and even hospice workers. The interactions with these clinicians will focus on the needs of the patient as someone in need of intervention; after all, the purpose of medical intervention is to prolong life and provide comfort, and the clinicians will have a goal of leaving the patient feeling better at the end of any intervention than they were at the beginning. Unfortunately, these services require an assessment of the patient's various capacities, and that means a focus on what is lacking, not what still works. Focusing on what doesn't work distorts the holistic picture of the patient into a negative framework, and that feeds back into their mind-set, producing a negative perception of their well-being. For me, every time I went to see a clinician I felt worse. As I said in an e-mail to a friend in December 2015:

> *The management of a terminal illness means recurring contact with clinicians, and I have deduced that there is a reflexivity to this process. The more contact you have with people concerned about your deteriorating condition – the worse you feel. Give me a day in the*

garden and I feel good. Give me a visit from the hospice
nurse or a respiratory specialist and I feel flat and
exhausted.

That's not the same as saying these people are problematic, quite the contrary, they are wonderful and professional. The issue here is my perception. The contacts impact negatively on me, no matter what benefits emerge, and it's made worse because I have contact with at least eight different specialisms working as part of a multi-disciplinary team (neurologist, respiratory technician, respiratory doctor, dietician, speech and language therapist, occupational health technicians, orthotic and hospice specialists), as well as carers. In a period of just a month that's a lot of occasions for triggering a dip in how I feel. The shift in perception is compounded by time taken preparing for the visit, during the visit, and reflecting on the outcomes of the visit. On the other hand, it would be foolish to deny the reality of a declining capability, and if these visits bring me close to tears, that may be no bad thing to help balance the emotions. There are several ideas going around on the health benefits of crying to relieve stress and improve mood.

I can see no ready solution to this problem. The work of the clinicians is critical to my well-being, and the frequency of the visits linked to a degrading body is also important. My friend's experience of breast cancer care meant they had a single point of contact with clinical services – a so called 'care navigator' – and this has been suggested for MND sufferers. In practise, a single clinician with all the requisite skills would be expensive, and I could not justify that cost against my perceptions of just being a bit glum because I have more conversations.

The second reflexive trigger relates to loss of capacity. I'm reminded of Tony Hancock's blood donor sketch, where he's giving a pint of blood and describes it as being 'a whole armful'. It's not, or course, because the blood is taken from the system as a whole, and there's still blood left in the arm after the donation (donation meant so much more in the days when profit had no part to play in giving blood). But Hancock's description is how we look at loss of capacity; something has been removed from the whole, and it needs to be quantified. My diary is full of comments about losing strength, or capacity for talking, breathing, swallowing, lifting, and walking. Every time I sense a loss, something disappears, and yet, after losing so much capacity I'm still sitting here, just managing to write this paragraph. There are different forces at work and the straightforward loss does not take account of the body's ability to compensate, nor the mind's ability to adapt to the loss. Again, taking an extract from my diary in December 2015, I was so specific that I wrote:

It's been the second significant quick 'drop' in performance. Both the last week of October and now this week (third week December) have both had similar symptoms akin to feeling internal chemical activity (heat), accompanied by tiredness and the subsequent loss of physical capacity. I would guess I lost 10% of my previous strength this week, a capacity already reduced so perhaps not fully 10% of my pre MND capacity, but maybe 5% of it.

Looking back on this it would seem that I had several regular periods where I lost limb capacity, but I had the nouse to understand that a drop on a previous drop was not a 10% loss each time. The problem of quantifying the perceived loss is that there are no easy waypoints, or markers. Loss cannot be quantified so readily, it's just a feeling. What makes it worse is that degradation is not limited to a single element of the body. For me, there are separate elements affecting swallowing, neck strength, arm and leg strength and breathing. These elements lose capacity at different times, and that increases my perception of overall loss. Sometimes it feels almost overwhelming and it's hard to get a clear picture of what's going on. If I totalled up all the perceptions of loss in my diary, I calculate I would have been dead months ago, and yet I'm still pressing the keys on my laptop.

The body compensates for these losses by doing things differently. Moving and eating are just two examples of adaptation. Moving is slower, with a reduced span of actions, but these still enable the basic jobs to get done. Eating may take four times longer and requires food to be cut up small or liquidised, but the fuel is still taken on board. Certainly the taste of a good bottle of Sancerre is marred by the degradation, but my body says that's no longer important. Turning over in bed was a problem a year ago, but with a hospital style adjustable bed and satin pyjamas it's as easy to slide around now as it was many months back. The mind adapts too. Where mobility makes it difficult getting the tea out of the cupboard, the tea caddy now sits full time on the worktop; the difficult work is removed. The building and the furniture can also be better adapted. Where hands are less effective they are supported by shoulders (literally; putting the shoulder to the wheel), but it made sense for me to give up driving and using a chainsaw many months ago. These tasks would be just too risky. New knowledge adds intellectual capacity at the same time as losing physical capacity; it's not resilience in the full sense of 'bouncing back', but there is a compensatory element dampening the full impact of decline.

This is not linked to the concept of fighting the disease or being heroic (the single most disappointing misuse of a term in our current media); it's just a realisation that, like a visit from a clinician, perception is often worse than reality, and despite the miserable diagnosis, there is a good deal of positivity to be had from understanding how a debilitating disease misrepresents itself in the mind. The consequence of this discovery for me is that whilst decline is no friend, it can be seen as a false image. Odysseus didn't succumb to the Siren's call, and similarly I stop myself being at the mercy of misunderstanding mental and physical weaknesses, and I make sure I remember the adaptations and compensations that help me along the way. I recognise my analysis here might be viewed as speaking from a position of strength, and although I challenge criticism that mine is a privileged view, I accept that I am well looked after.

Reflections

Epicurus did not just pronounce on death, he pronounced on life too; saying that it should be full of friendship and the good things of life. Epicureanism is often associated with good food and drink, but that is not his primary message. He said friendship 'dances around the world', is the greatest means of attaining pleasure, and it provides the greatest security. Long before the bible's New Testament was written, he said friends have to treat each other as well as they treat themselves. My dying is made easier by having the support of a close and loving family, something I know many people don't have. I've also got good friends, locally, and spread throughout the world, who I can talk with face to face, or through my preferred medium of e-mail, where I don't have to struggle with talking. I can spend my days linked electronically with messages from friends, and spend evenings filled with family stories, shared memories, or spontaneous exchanges about nothing much at all. It doesn't get any better than that, it just doesn't.

I was born in 1954 CE, a fourth child for my parents, and from Anglo-Saxon, and a bit of Celtic stock (although the Celts were just an earlier phase of Germanic migration). In the big scheme of things I am the product of at least 100 million successful reproductions without a single break in the ancestral chain, or otherwise I wouldn't be here. Perhaps only the last six generations of that chain have been recorded. The last link looks something like me, and it's not for me to say if evolution did well, made a good fist of the linkages, or had a poor school report. It doesn't matter; this is, or was, me.

I consider myself to have been more *tabula rasa* (blank slate) than most, because I was brought up in a house with few books, and my parents (probably still suffering from the shock of the Second World War) expressed little in the way of social or political analysis. I was therefore moulded by friends and relationships more than history and tradition. I have been fortunate to find all my friendships faithful and loving. I am a Humean Epicurean; Epicurean first, because my life is defined best by these friendships, and Humean second, because I believe that emotions define us better than reason. To me the combination of these two beliefs screams humanity. It allows love, passion, and learning to thrive. It allows tribalism to work with individualism to enable both freedom and security. I've never had to go off to fight a war, and on my way through life I was fortunate to acquire a PhD in the teaching of creativity. Poignantly, my graduation was a month after my MND diagnosis. As Bertrand Russell suggested, I've tried to pursue knowledge and kindliness and live with hope, and I've had sufficient courage of my convictions to stand for parliament. As for writing this book, the work of reading, thinking and typing put me in a bubble where I felt no adverse symptoms, and it was a good place.

Neurologist Dr Allan Ropper says in his book *Reaching Down the Rabbit Hole* 'only the nicest people get ALS [MND].' It's probably not at all true, but it's good to see it in print. My wife Helen and I have enjoyed an extraordinarily happy marriage, and we've got two amazing daughters, Holly and Sophie who, unsurprisingly, both turned out to be scientists. My only unfulfilled wish was to care for Helen until she died, and that's what tugs the emotions most. It's not incommunicable, on the contrary; but I'm sorry and sad I can't do that.

At the outset of this book I planned to give an interpretation of death untainted by religious superstitious and I've enjoyed exploring the topic. Perhaps I wanted to give myself a 'shot of courage' to overcome the difficulties I face in the coming weeks, or perhaps it was to help me be resilient, even if there's no recovery. Perhaps it will help my family and friends respond more easily to my condition and my death, and I hope I've given food for thought to other readers. My next steps are clear; as John Lennon says 'Life is what happens to you while you're busy making other plans.' I don't need to know how it ends, and like a good book, there will be loose ends for others to pick up to build a new narrative. I wish them great adventures. There are no more milestones for me to hit, except my own cue for 'exeunt stage left'. I am comfortable to share with Epicurus his views that life is about love, friendships and shared experiences, and not about greed, money or power. This book is dedicated to the nuclear family that lit up my world, and I thank all the family and friends who have shone their light into my life. It's been a gas.

References

Notes

The acronym B.C.E stands for Before the Common Era and is a non-religious dating convention that substitutes the traditional dating of BC and AD (Before Christ and Anno Domini meaning 'in the year of our lord'). Dates traditionally labelled AD (a system that was started in 525CE on the Black Sea coast of what is now Romania and Bulgaria) are now labelled CE (Common Era). It's not a new convention; it's been around for 300 years and it was used by Jewish academics 150 years ago. The rise of secularism has made it more popular.

Albom, M. (1997) *Tuesdays with Morrie: an old man, a young man, and life's greatest lesson.* New York: Doubleday,

ALS Association (n.d.) *Criteria for diagnosis.* Available at: http://www.alsa.org/als-care/resources/publications-videos/factsheets/criteria-for-diagnosis.html and

http://www.alsa.org/about-als/what-is-als.html.

Banville, J. (2005) *The Sea.* London: Picador.

Barnes, J. (2009) *Nothing to be Frightened of.* London: Random House.

Bathes, R. (2000) *Mourning Diary.* New York: Hill & Wang.

Blom, P. (2011) *Wicked Company: Freethinkers and Friendship in Pre-Revolutionary France.* London: Phoenix.

Callanan, M. & Kelley, P. (1992) *Final Gifts: Understanding and Helping the Dying.* London: Hodder & Stoughton.

Camus, A. (1971) *The Rebel.* Harmondsworth: Penguin.

Clark, M. (1977) *Antonio Gramsci and the Revolution that Failed.* London: Yale University Press.

Dante Alighieri (1971/1320) *The Divine Comedy. Vol 1 Inferno.* Harmondsworth: Penguin Books Ltd.

De Beauvoir, S. (1969) *A Very Easy Death.* Aylesbury: Penguin Books.

Didion, J. (2006) *The Year of Magical Thinking.* London: Fourth Estate.

Durkheim, E. (1933/1984) *The Division of Labour in Society.* New York: Macmillan.

Gawande, A. (2014) *Being mortal: medicine and what matters in the end.* New York: Metropolitan Books.

Graves, R. (1955) *The Greek Myths.* Aylesbury: Penguin Books.

Haidt, J. (2012) *The Righteous Mind: Why Good People Are Divided By Politics and Religion.* London: Penguin Books.

Harris, R. (2013) *An Officer and a Spy*. London: Hutchinson.

Hesiod, (1988/Eighth Century BCE) *Theogony*. Oxford: OUP.

Hume, D. (1739/1962) *A Treatise of Human Nature*. Glasgow: William Collins Sons & Co Ltd.

Kahneman, D. (2011) *Thinking Fast and Slow*. London: Allen Lane.

Kalanithi, P. (2016) *When Breath Becomes Air*. London: Bodley Head.

Kübler-Ross E. (1969) *On Death and Dying*. New York: Routledge.

Lewis, C. S. (1968). *A grief observed*. London, Faber & Faber.

Locke, J. (1690) *An Essay concerning Human Understanding*. Available at:
http://www2.hn.psu.edu/faculty/jmanis/locke/humanund.pdf (last accessed 4th January 2016).

Lucretius (1994/1951) *On the Nature of Things*, (translation by R. E. Latham), Harmondsworth: Penguin Books.

Motor Neurone disease Association website. Available at: http://www.mndassociation.org/

Mylastsong. Available at
http://www.mylastsong.com/advice/461/109/care/a-death-plan-for-the-end-of-life-experience-you-want (last accessed 18th September 2016).

Neudert C., Oliver D., Wasner M., and Borasio G. (2001) *The course of the terminal phase in patients with amyotrophic lateral sclerosis.* J Neurol. 2001 Jul; 248(7): 612-6.

Nuland, S. (1994) *How we Die.* London: Chatto & Windus.

North, D. (1990) *Institutions, Institutional Change and Economic Performance.* New York: Cambridge University Press.

O'Keefe, T. (2009) *Epicureanism.* Los Angeles: UC Press.

Paine, T. (2004/1794) *The Age of Reason.* New York: Dover Publications.

Picardie, R. (1997) *Before I say Goodbye.* London: Penguin Books

Pink, D. (2009) *The Puzzle of Motivation.* Available at: http://www.ted.com/talks/dan_pink_on_motivation? language=en

Polanyi, M. (1958) *Personal Knowledge: Towards a Post-Critical Philosophy.* London: Routledge and Kegan Paul.

Ropper, A. & Burrell, D. (2015) *Reaching Down the Rabbit Hole.* London: Atlantic Books.

Strayed, C. (2012) *Wild.* New York: Alfred A. Knopf.

Sunstein, C. & Thaler, R. (2009) *Nudge.* New Haven, Conn: Yale University Press.

Taylor, C. (2016) *Dying: A Memoir.* Melbourne: Text Publishing.

Tooby, J. & Cosmides, L. (1992) The Psychological Foundations of Culture. In Barkow, J.H., Tooby, J. & Cosmides, L. (Eds.) (1992) *The Adapted Mind; Evolutionary Psychology and the Generation of Culture.* Oxford: Oxford University Press.

Verhaeghe, P. (2014) *What About Me? The Struggle for Identity in a Market-based Society.* London: Scribe Publications Pty Ltd.

Weber, M. (1964, first published 1922) *The Theory of Social and Economic Organisation.* London: Free Press.

Yalomb, I. (2008) *Staring at the Sun: Overcoming the Dread of Death.* London: Piatkus.